...team Pac...
...ANY.
...d IRELAND
...L SERVICE
...A
...KINGSTOWN
...ASSENGER ROUTE.

...n Screw Steamers
...ER," "MUNSTER"
... 3,000 Tons, 9,000
... 24 Knots, sail twice

First published 2018 by
Elm Books
Dublin
Ireland

info@elmbooks.ie

www.elmbooks.ie

ISBN: 978-0-9931989-5-3

Copyright for text © Carmel Uí Cheallaigh 2018

Copyright for illustrations © Jimmy Burns 2018

Design by Alan Nolan, alannolan.ie

All rights reserved. No part of this publication may be reproduced or utilised in any form or by any means, electronic or mechanical, including photocopying, recording or in any information storage and retrieval system, without permission in writing from the publisher.

Printing: KPS Colour Print, Knock, Co. Mayo, Ireland

CENTENARY COMMEMORATION

R.M.S. LEINSTER
10 · X · 18

THE FORGOTTEN TRAGEDY

Carmel Uí Cheallaigh

ILLUSTRATED BY **JIMMY BURNS**

ElmBooks

A special thank you to Philip Lecane
for his encouragement and expertise
from start to finish

The National Maritime Museum of Ireland

Today, old sailor Jim is taking his grandchildren Seán and Saoirse to visit the Maritime Museum in Dún Laoghaire.

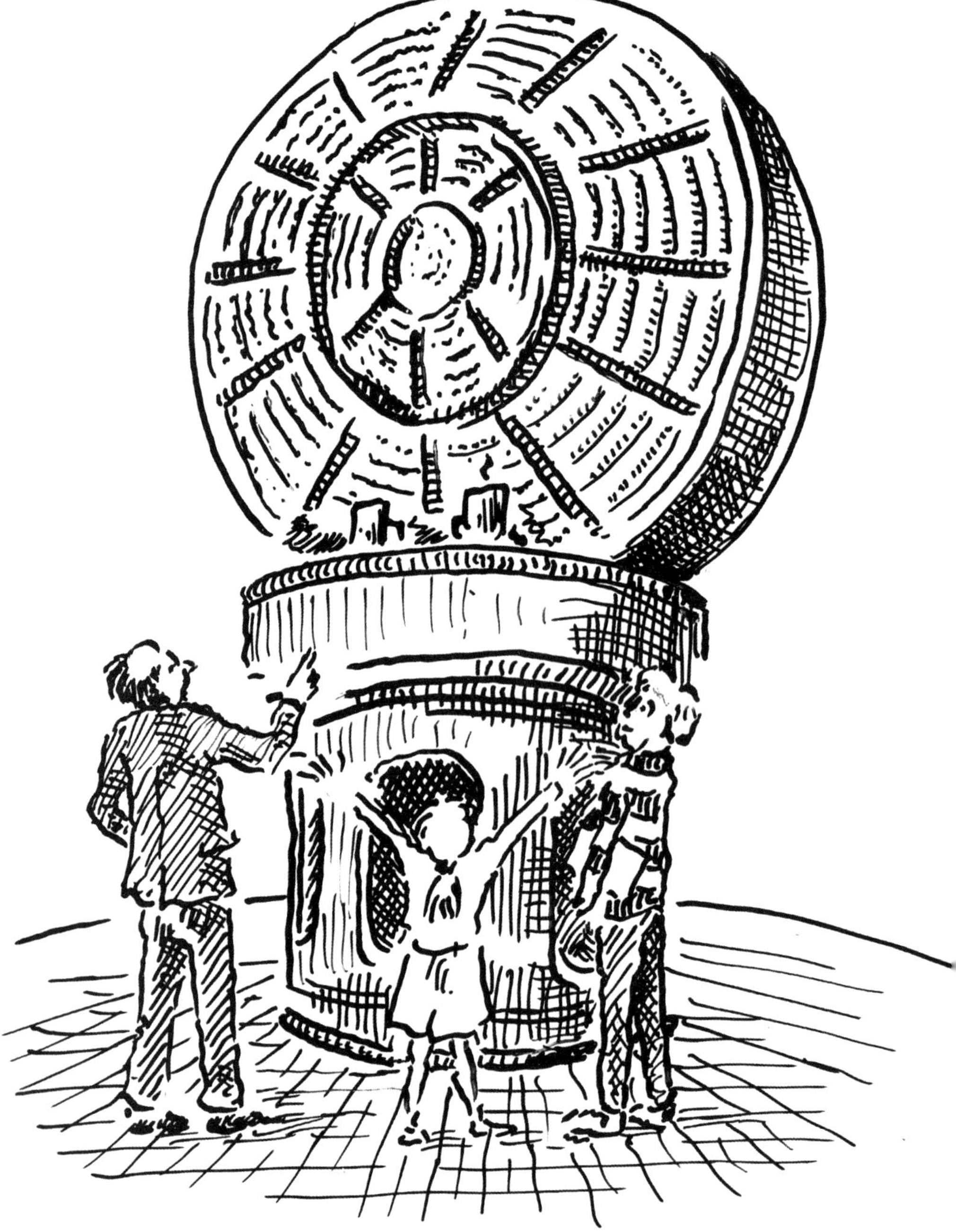

"This was once the Mariner's Church," he tells the children. "Officers and sailors prayed here before they set off on their travels. I often brought your daddy here when he was a chiseller."

Built in 1837, the Mariner's Church has been transformed into a fun, lively space, where you can learn everything you want to know about the sea.

There are all kinds of interesting things to look at: amazing artefacts, marvellous models, perfectly preserved photographs and exciting exhibitions.

"Follow me," Grandad beckons. "Oh, look – this ship here sank 100 years ago this year. Let's find out more about it."

RMS Leinster

The Royal Mail Steam-ship **Leinster** was one of four identical ships, all named after the Irish provinces, the others were the **RMS Ulster**, **RMS Munster** and **RMS Connaught**.

The **RMS Leinster** set sail for the first time in September 1896, launched by the City of Dublin Steam Packet Company.

It was one of the fastest cross channel steamers in the world at the time. It travelled between Kingstown (Dún Laoghaire) and Holyhead in North Wales in just 2^1/$_2$ hours, carrying passengers and lots of bags of mail.

"Once, I went from Dún Laoghaire to Holyhead," Seán tells his grandfather. "I was on my way to a football tournament in Manchester."

Mail and passengers were carried back and forth across the Irish Sea twice every day. Twenty-two General Post Office postal workers sorted the 250 mailbags on board.

They had to work speedily as the boat travelled along. In fact, they worked so fast that, in 1918, a letter posted in Dublin could arrive in London the following day.

Mail trains met the mail boats at the Carlisle Pier in Kingstown and Admiralty Pier in Holyhead, carrying post and passengers on to their destinations.

The introduction of the Penny Black postage stamp in 1840 made it possible for more people to post letters as it was cheap and people could afford it.

World War 1 made mail even more important as the telegraph was too expensive and communication by radio could be listened in to by soldiers and spies.

During 1917 and 1918, the **Leinster** carried many soldiers to and from England as they travelled onwards to the battlefields of France and Belgium.

Ship Design

"Look, here's the model of the actual ship," Grandad points out.

The **Leinster** had three main decks, with the lowest housing the postal sorting office.

The first-class dining room was on the middle deck. Here, they could seat 79 people at seven tables at any given time.

The upper deck, known as the promenade deck, was the only place on the ship where you could walk outside.

There was a dumbwaiter lift to take the meals down from the ship's galley to the dining areas.

Above the upper deck was a boat deck where the lifeboats were stored.

"We did a project on the **Titanic** at school, Grandad," Saoirse says, "it sounds exactly like that."

"Yes," he replies, "the **Titanic** and the **Lusitania** were also Royal Mail ships."

The Captain and Crew

The Captain of the **Leinster**, William Birch, was born in Dublin in 1857. He started his career when most ships were powered by sail rather than steam. He and his wife Louisa had 10 children, seven born in England and three in Ireland. Throughout his career, the family moved between Liverpool, Kingstown and Holyhead. He began working with the City of Dublin Steam Packet Company, which owned the **Leinster**, in 1902.

The ship had a crew of 77 and most of them were Irish and Welsh. These included officers who helped Captain Birch to navigate the ship — that is to see it was going the right way — and organise everybody on board.

While the officers worked up on the bridge, the high part near the front of the ship, the engineering crew worked down below the ordinary decks in the engine room. They had a much noisier, dirtier job. Stokers shovelled coal into the ship's furnace, which boiled up water until the steam this created drove the engines, which turned the propellers and pushed the ship through the water. Greasers kept the ship's mighty steam engine and many other machines on board oiled.

Up on the decks above all that noise, the stewards and stewardesses worked hard at their housekeeping jobs, making sure the passengers and crew were comfortable and fed.

The Towns of Kingstown and Holyhead

Kingstown (which we now call Dún Laoghaire) was a very busy place. Travel to and from Dún Laoghaire became much easier when the first railway was built there in 1834 and the big Carlisle Pier was built in 1856, making it easier and safer for ships to dock.

In 1918, around 17,000 people lived in Kingstown. Sadly, many were sick that year, and quite a few died from what became known as Spanish Flu.

George's Street was Kingstown's main shopping area. Grocers and drapers sold food and clothes. Customers could buy everything from freshly caught fish to fine silk.

There were plenty of things to do. Locals and tourists enjoyed the Picture House cinema where Charlie Chaplin was popular, the Pavilion Concert Hall and Gardens, the new Carnegie Library and the swimming baths. Many different hotels catered for visitors, including Ross's in Mellifont Avenue, which was especially popular with mail boat passengers.

Holyhead and Ireland have always had a special connection. It was the first stop for many Irish emigrants when they left the country and the last when they returned home for visits.

In 1918, Holyhead had a population of 10,500. Most of these were Welsh and spoke the Welsh language rather than English. "What's the Welsh language like Grandad?" Saoirse asks.

"It's another great Celtic language, like Irish," he answers. "Welsh children learn it at school and they speak it in loads of towns throughout Wales."

Unfortunately, in 1918, lots of people in Holyhead had tuberculosis (TB), a deadly infectious disease which killed many of them. To make matters worse, there was food rationing there because of the War. Many people were ill and hungry in Holyhead, so times were tough in 1918.

Despite this, the town was full of activity. There were pubs, cinemas, and many community events. People from the country villages came in to the town to do their shopping.

The War

Between 1914 and 1918, Britain was at war with Germany. France, Russia, Italy and the United States were on Britain's side. Many Irish people joined up with the British Armed Forces as there were very few jobs in Ireland at the time and many Irish people were very poor.

In World War 1, U Boats were the big new threat. These were submarines that could hide under water and blow up ships using torpedoes, explosives they could fire under the sea without warning.

Although the **Leinster** relied on its speed to avoid submarines, it was also armed with a light machinegun for extra protection. Three gunners, or specially trained sailors, operated the gun.

The Wrens, or Women's Royal Naval Service, was formed less than a year before. Its members carried out Royal Navy work on shore but sometimes travelled between ports on the boats that sailed between Kingstown and Holyhead.

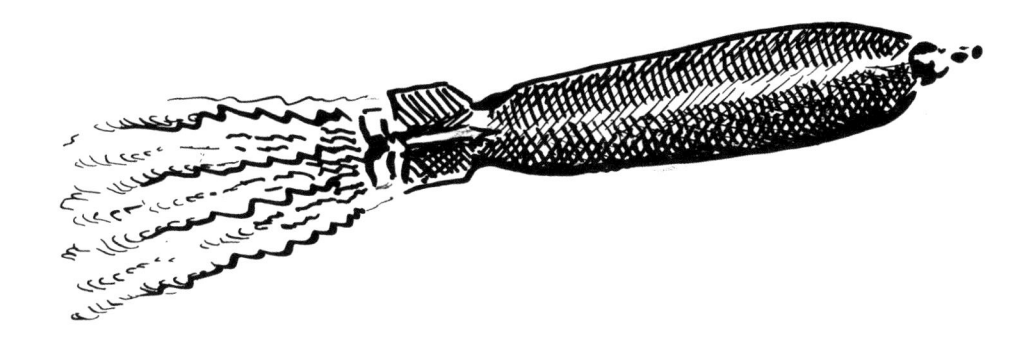

On 6 October, the German government wrote to Woodrow Wilson, the US president, asking for a truce, on land, in the sea and in the air.

"That truce would not be signed for another five weeks, children," Grandad sighs.

Disaster Strikes

On Thursday morning, 10 October, 1918, the crew of the **Leinster** prepared as normal to travel. Five-hundred soldiers were on board, some with their families, returning from leave.

The ship was so full that many other passengers who wanted to travel that day could not get aboard.

At 8.50am, the ship chugged out from the Carlisle Pier in Kingstown. The weather was fine but the sea was rough. A crewman on board later reported that there was a fresh breeze and a heavy sea running, which increased as the ship got further out from land.

Lying in wait, was the German submarine UB-123. Seven miles out, just beyond the Kish Light Vessel, it fired three torpedoes. The first missed the **Leinster**. The second hit it near the postal sorting office, killing 21 of the 22 postal workers working there, and smashing the ship's hull.

At this stage, Captain Birch ordered all hands to the boat stations. He wanted to turn the ship back to Kingstown but a third torpedo hit, causing an explosion that killed most of the others on board.

The whole attack lasted less than eight minutes. An SOS message had been sent after the first torpedo struck.

"Look, children," points Grandad. "This diagram shows us all about the rescue operation."

RESCUE SHIP	NUMBER OF PEOPLE RESCUED
HMS Mallard	19 men, 2 women
HMS Lively	102 men, 14 women, 1 child
HMS Seal	51 survivors, 2 bodies

After the Attack

Many people drowned or died from hypothermia, or cold, while waiting to be rescued. The official death toll was 501 but recent research suggests that more than 560 lives were lost, the greatest ever loss of life in the Irish Sea.

People back on shore searched frantically for their loved ones as the bodies taken from the sea were unloaded at the Victoria Wharf in Kingstown.

The majority of the civilian survivors were taken to St Michael's Hospital in Dún Laoghaire and to local hotels. Soldiers were brought to several military hospitals around the city.

Many civilians were buried in Deansgrange, Glasnevin and Mount Jerome cemeteries in Dublin. More were buried in other cemeteries around the country. The bodies of people who were not Irish were taken to cemeteries in their home countries.

About 150 of the soldiers, sailors and airmen who died were buried at the Grangegorman Military Cemetery, Dublin.

Josephine Carr, a 19-year-old shorthand typist, from Cork, was the first Wren to die on active service when the **Leinster** was torpedoed.

Captain Birch had supervised the lowering of the lifeboats until he was blown off the bridge. His lifeboat later capsized. His body was never found.

"Who was on the submarine that fired the torpedoes, Grandad?" Seán asks. "What happened to them?"

"Tap on this screen," says Grandad, "and find out all about them."

Robert Ramm was the Captain of UB-123. He was born on 3 December, 1890 in Mecklenburg, Germany. He and his wife Gerda had a son and a daughter. UB-123 was sunk eight days after the attack on the **Leinster**, when it struck a mine, off the Scottish coast. All 36 young crewmen on board were killed.

Remembering the Leinster

In November 1991, one of the **Leinster's** anchors was raised from the seabed. On 29 January, 1996, the newly cleaned anchor was unveiled at a special ceremony attended by friends and relatives of **Leinster** passengers.

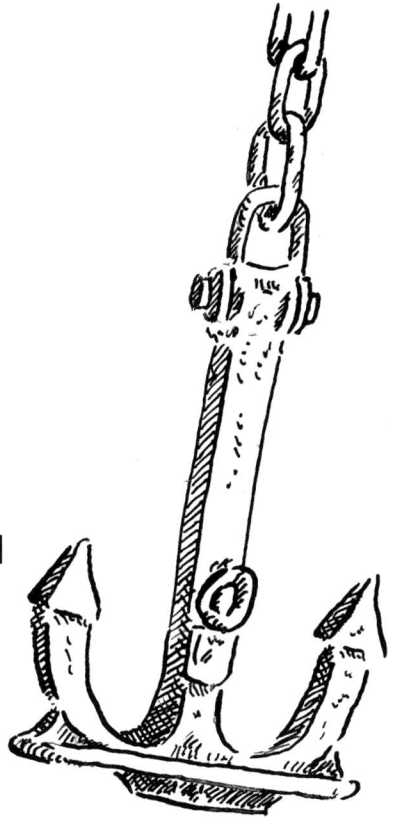

Two further **RMS Leinster** commemorations were held in Dún Laoghaire and Holyhead in 2003 and 2008. Also, in 2008 a special **Leinster** stamp was issued by the Irish Post Office.

"You know, children, many relatives of the people who died on the **Leinster** still live in Dún Laoghaire, Holyhead and beyond.

"There were people from Australia, New Zealand, Britain, Canada and the United States on board too. Indeed, we would not be standing here today if my father, your great grandfather, was not one of the 50 fortunate people who didn't get a ticket to travel on the **Leinster** on that fateful morning as it was already full. He told me that story many times, as it was a lucky escape for him and the others who were left behind."

RMS Leinster Quiz

Q Where can you learn everything about the sea?

A

Q Who owned the **Leinster**?

A

Q Where was the **Leinster** going?

A

Q Name two other Royal Mail Ships

A

Q Who was the Captain of the **Leinster** and where was he born?

A

Q Who was the president of the United States in 1918?

A

Q On what date was the **Leinster** sunk?

A

Q Where was it when it was attacked?

A

Q What country's submarine sank the **Leinster**?

A

Q How many torpedoes were fired?

A

Q What was a Wren and who was the first Wren to die on active service?

A

Q Who was the captain of UB-123 and where was he born?

A

Q Name the Dublin cemeteries where civilians were buried

A

Q Name the Dublin cemeteries where soldiers were buried

A

RMS Leinster
• Quiz •

More Books by Carmel Uí Cheallaigh

Spidey
ISBN: 9781899922840

Leanbh Nua
ISBN: 9781899922963

An Tolg Draíochta
ISBN: 9780993198908

The New Cat
ISBN: 9780993198922

Man of the People
Fr William Doyle SJ
ISBN: 9780993198939

www.carmelsbooks.com

40
35
30
I R I S
The Skerries
Light Ho.
West Mouse
Pt. Carmel
HOLYHEAD BAY
Holyhead
Harbour
1
3
5
Llanfair
Llanfaelog
C A E R N
EXPLANATION
County Town as BEAUMARIS
Market Towns